MW01701995

Ordinary Christians, Extraordinary Mission

Meditations on the Work of Christ

Belong!

neighbors loving neighbors

Scriptures taken from the Holy Bible, New International Version®, NIV®. Copyright ©1973, 1978, 1984, 2011 by Biblica, Inc.™ Used by permission of Zondervan. All rights reserved worldwide. www.zondervan.com

The "NIV" and "New International Version" are trademarks registered in the United States Patent and Trademark Office by Biblica, Inc.™

©2019 Cindy Fisher
Published by Belong!, 124 Park St., NE, Vienna, VA 22180
Cover and Layout by Derek Adam Thomas, with Yaneisy K. Martinez.

CONTENTS

FOREWORD
Called to Belong!

...and he sent them out to proclaim the kingdom of God and to heal the sick.
— Luke 9:2

For Jesus, word and action came together as He addressed both spiritual and physical needs to transform people's lives. And as remarkable as it is to witness personal healing from the inside out, God's redemptive purpose transcends the individual and transforms communities. God's aim is to reconcile the entire world to Himself (2 Cor 5:18–20; Eph 2:16; Col 1:20–21). He is bringing heaven and earth back into full alignment.

In Vienna, Virginia, a socially and economically diverse group of local churches and community members came together to discuss the current state of affairs in town—both the blessings and the brokenness—and to imagine how things might look different if God's will were actually done on earth as it is in heaven. Then these neighbors began working together to address issues raised in those discussions, such as access to employment, healthy food, education, transportation, and opportunities for spiritual growth. These efforts are the antecedents of BELONG! Vienna, an expression of the Body of Christ; neighbors organized to love their fellow neighbors in very practical ways.

While the effort was conceived as Christian outreach, an early and frequent step in the process must be what Cindy Fisher calls "in-reach," meaning our own deep reflection on God's call to service, and on the manner in which His call shapes our motivations and the desired outcomes of our work in the community. This series of 32 meditations is a compilation of weekly devotions written for members of the outreach teams and interested members of the broader community. We are pleased to share them with you through this book, and to invite you to consider, through these pages, where you belong in the Work of Christ in your community.

Grace and peace,

Pastor David Jordan-Haas
BELONG! Vienna

FOREWORD
Spending Ourselves

When Cindy Fisher asked me to write a foreword to her new devotional booklet, I was honored. Cindy is a good friend and a wonderful person with a missionary heart. More importantly, over a decade ago, Cindy was one of the key catalysts in a movement that revolutionized Columbia's global mission enterprise.

Like many churches over the last two decades or so, Columbia's denominationally-centered model of "paying and praying" for missions and missionaries had long been obsolete. However, an interim solution of "partnering and playing" was not the answer. While we were sending many Columbians to the field as one or two week "vacationaries," we were not making significant impacts. Our efforts were far more focused on the needs of our church and volunteers than on seeing results in the field. We were spending vast quantities of money getting people to people and places of great need, but we were barely putting a dent in the need. Christ was not honored in this, and we knew it. We were spending, but poverty was not ending. We needed to move to a model of "partnering and participation."

After months of prayer and deliberation, we knew we were being called to change our approach toward the last, least, and lost of the world. Sometime during that period of seeking God's will, Cindy was given a Scripture from Isaiah 58:10: [The Lord says] "And if you spend yourselves in behalf of the hungry and satisfy the needs of the oppressed, then your light will rise in the darkness, and your night will become like the noonday." We knew immediately this was a revelation from God, and we established our "Spend Yourself" mission of "feeding people physically and spiritually in the name of Christ through long-term relationship and development."

Over the course of a decade, Columbia has invested over $7 million in development efforts locally, in Southwest Virginia, in Haiti, and in India, and the sky is still the limit. Our focus has been on yielding our own needs to those we were serving, and that has changed everything. In time, we established three criteria for every Columbia mission enterprise:

(1) Focused: doing it right rather than quick; (2) Transformative: output-based input; and (3) Just: our best for the others' good. Though Cindy was not with us for the whole journey, I am not sure it ever would have begun without her presence.

In the past decade, communities have been transformed, and so have we. We have seen human beings moved from extreme poverty and dependence to well-being and self-sufficiency, from hopelessness to hope. And we have seen many come to Christ in the process, simply because they have seen how we and God loved them. We have been used essentially by God in this process as we have "Spent Ourselves," but those we have served no longer need us to ensure that their communities and families prosper. In each instance, "Spending Ourselves" has meant working ourselves out of a job, and that has been our goal all along.

Spend Yourself has been one of the most rewarding journeys of my life, and it has only just begun. I wish every church and Christian could understand the joy and efficacy of catalyzing global development and partnering with indigenous churches in the process. To my thinking, every successful church will eventually discover this model. God used Cindy and some other key leaders to help us find the way sooner than later, and I am forever grateful to her. I commend her thoughts to you without reservation. Fair warning: they are more revolutionary than you might yet realize.

Dr. Jim Baucom, Senior Pastor
Columbia Baptist Church
Falls Church, Virginia

PREFACE

When we think about missions, we tend to think about the outward components: the people being reached, the need being met, the plan being implemented, the results being attained. But the truth is that the outward mission is only one-half of a whole. For every outward mission there is an at-least-equal inward mission: an answer to God's call, a step of faith being taken, a deepening understanding of who God is, an increasingly Christ-centered and Christ-reflecting life. When we understand that every call from God inherently encompasses an inward as well as an outward journey—not only for each person, individually, but also for the team, the church, or the collection of churches being called—we can better prepare for, nurture, and celebrate both.

To that end, these devotions were originally written in support of Belong!, a local missions initiative spearheaded by Vienna Presbyterian Church with the aim of encouraging spiritual, physical, and economic well-being. The intent of the devotions, which were disseminated on a weekly basis, was to initiate an inward journey that would feed into the outward journey, thereby creating a virtuous cycle.

The devotions, themselves, are the result of just such a virtuous cycle, significantly drawing on my experience as lay leader for Spend Yourself®, a missions program developed by Columbia Baptist Church to address physical and spiritual hunger. As lay leader, I spent more than five years immersed in Isaiah 58, the chapter in which Spend Yourself is rooted (particularly verse 10). This immersion, in combination with the work carried out by the Spend Yourself team, was deeply transformational, certainly for me and I hope for all involved. The devotions herein reflect my attempt to capture and share, at least in part, that inward journey.

I am greatly indebted to Vienna Presbyterian Church—in particular, David Jordan-Haas, Senior Associate Pastor for Congregational Care and Outreach; Glenda Simpkins Hoffman, Associate Pastor for Spiritual Formation; Sue Hamblen, Director of Missions; and Phil Covell, former Belong! Project Manager—for entrusting me with the writing of these devotions. I am also deeply appreciative of the time and attention that Phil Covell and Scott Slocum gave to reviewing each week's devotion prior to dissemination, and for providing the driving force behind the publication of this final devotional.

The depth of my gratitude to God and to Columbia Baptist Church for the opportunity to serve as Spend Yourself lay leader exceeds my capabilities of expression. To serve alongside James Baucom, Senior Pastor; Greg Loewer,

Pastor for Missions; Anne Tomas, former Pastor for Missions; every single member of the amazing Spend Yourself team; all of the pastors and staff across the church, who worked to integrate Spend Yourself into their various activities and programs; and the church as a whole, without whom nothing would have been accomplished, was a source of great joy and an experience that I will forever treasure. Spend Yourself was not just something they did, but epitomizes who they were and are.

I also give my heartfelt thanks to my husband and children, who are my heart and joy. It's true that when one member of the family serves in missions, the whole family serves. The time required to establish Spend Yourself was considerable, especially early on. I will forever be grateful for the support they gave and the sacrifices they made. And last but definitely not least, I wish to thank my parents, who provided the critical foundation on which everything else has been built, and my sister, whose deep faith has long been an inspiration.

To learn more about Belong!, go to https://viennapres.org/viennaoutreach/.
To learn more about Spend Yourself®, go to https://www.columbiabaptist.org/care-and-help/feeding-the-hungry/.

INTRODUCTION

"Love the Lord your God with all your heart and with all your soul and with all your strength" (Deut. 6:5) and "Love your neighbor as yourself" (Lev. 19:18). These commands permeate the bible, threading their way from one book to the next, one century to the next, one generation to the next. Rooted in the Spirit, they escape the confines of printed page and embed themselves in our hearts, binding our lives to those who preceded us; adding our stories to those of old; creating out of our diversity of experience, thought, and ability a unity of purpose; and most of all, drawing us ever closer to the One who first loved us and lays claim to our lives. More than just words on a page or boxes to check, they brim with the essence of who God is and who we're meant to be. In their simple but enduring truth, the fullness of life is found.

But what does it mean to love God? What does it mean to love our neighbors? What tangible difference do these commands make in our lives? If love permeated every moment of our days, how would our lives be different? How would our families be different? How would our communities be different? How would the world be different?

God is calling each and every one of us to follow him, not just when we first become Christians or in our spare time, not just when we're in church or on a summer mission project, but every single moment of every single day. We may be ordinary, everyday Christians, but he invites us, beseeches us, to join him in his extraordinary mission. The only question is, how will we respond?

Ordinary Christians, Extraordinary Mission comprises a series of devotions that journey into God's call to follow him, with the hope of deepening our relationship with God and with one another, and of strengthening our commitment to carrying out his work.

1

GOD'S TIMELESS CALL

The Lord had said to Abram, "Go from your country, your people, your father's household to the land I will show you."
—Genesis 12:1

God's call to Abram (not yet Abraham) to leave his home and travel to a new land wasn't simply a change of scenery. God was calling Abram to leave his comfort zone and enter the faith zone. In making the choice to follow God's call, Abram was placing his life in God's hands.

God continues to call us today, individually and collectively. He calls us on a journey that requires us to leave behind our comfort zones and step into the faith zone, to place our lives in his hands. He calls us to a Promised Land where he intends for us to be a blessing and to be blessed, but only if we, like Abram, choose to follow him.

For most of us, the Promised Land to which we're called doesn't require a literal journey. Just the act of opening ourselves to God's call, to seeing the world through his eyes, reveals the Promised Land before us. We step into it the moment we step out of our doors each day. It is our neighborhoods, our schools, our places of work, our communities. We are his missionaries-in-place. Every interaction becomes an opportunity to be his ambassadors, representing him through our attitudes, words, and actions. We may be ordinary, everyday Christians, but God calls us to an extraordinary mission. The Promised Land awaits!

Almighty God—You call each of us into a life's journey with you, a journey that requires us to leave our comfort zones and enter the faith zone. Through your call you give us an incomparable blessing, to be able to work hand-in-glove with you to carry out your mission. Along the way, challenges will come, possibly even significant tests of our faith, but we know that, through you, all obstacles are overcome. The Promised Land lies before us, on our doorsteps. Call us into it, oh Lord, and through all that we say and do, may you be glorified. In the name of our Lord and Savior, Jesus Christ, we pray. Amen.

2

FOLLOW THE LEADER

By day the Lord went ahead of them in a pillar of cloud to guide them on their way and by night in a pillar of fire to give them light, so that they could travel by day or night.
—Exodus 13:21

Do you remember playing the childhood game of follow the leader? It was impossible to know where the leader might go—through bushes, under fences, up trees. Not knowing and simply following was what made the game so much fun. In missions, God is our leader, and typically we know as little about what to expect as when playing the childhood game…often less. And if we're honest, we don't like it, and it's not fun. We'd much rather know in advance every step of the journey ahead, not to mention precise details about the destination to which we're headed. Otherwise, how can we be prepared? But God doesn't work that way. He wants us to rely wholly on him, one step at a time. Our groaning and complaining notwithstanding, he goes faithfully before us, steadfastly guiding us not only through the brightest sunshine of day, but also through the deepest, darkest depths of night. And just as he did for the Israelites, he will lead us to a place that we couldn't have begun to imagine, or find, on our own. With time and practice, we'll feel relieved to know that God is in control, in the lead. Eventually, when obstacles arise, our dismay and frustration will be offset by a sense of anticipation to see what God will do, and joy as we see paths made straight before him. And somewhere along the way, we'll realize that follow the Leader has become fun again.

Our Heavenly Father—How prone we are to going our own way. Even when we are carrying out your work, how often do we take it upon ourselves to figure out the path ahead, to make things happen the way we think they should happen? Forgive us for placing too much faith in ourselves and too little faith in you. Forgive us for our impatience. We thank you for your steadfast guidance, we praise you for your faithfulness to us, and we rejoice in the journey that lies before us and the destination to which you will lead us. In the name of our Lord and Savior, Jesus Christ, we pray. Amen.

God on Mission

3

FOR GOD SO LOVED THE WORLD

For God so loved the world that he gave his one and only Son,
that whoever believes in him shall not
perish but have eternal life.
—John 3:16

This is the core of the Christian faith. This gift of God's one and only son, Jesus Christ. Out of love, he came to a world that would reject him (John 1:9–11). Out of love, he sacrificed his life for the very people clamoring for his death (Romans 5:8). Out of love, he devoted himself to the mission set before him by God the Father (Philippians 2:6–8). What an outpouring of love! What a sacrifice! What a mission!

Yes, this is a missions story: a story of sharing the good news of God's mercy and grace; of feeding the hungry, healing the sick, and giving hope to the poor; of saving lives, for now and forever. Over the next few days we'll delve into the "heartset" of the one who is the example for all who follow him; the one who is the greatest missionary of all: God the Son, Jesus Christ.

Dear God, Our Father—Your saw us caught in the death-grip of sin, a vice from which we couldn't extricate ourselves, and because of your deep love for us, you couldn't bear to do nothing. In the face of our suffering, you acted, sending your one and only son to intercede personally, and at great cost, to secure not a quick fix, but a permanent solution—not because we deserve such a gift, but because of your deep love for each and every one of us. We thank you for your gift of hope, your gift of life. We thank you for the example that you have provided to us. And we praise you for your incomparable mercy, grace, and love. In the name of our Lord and Savior, Jesus Christ, we pray. Amen.

4

HERE AM I, SEND ME

In the beginning was the Word, and the Word was with God, and the Word was God. He was with God in the beginning. Through him all things were made; without him nothing was made that has been made.
—John 1:1-4

For you know the grace of our Lord Jesus Christ, that though he was rich, yet for your sake he became poor, so that you through his poverty might become rich.
—2 Corinthians 8:9

Isaiah spoke the powerful words, "Here am I. Send me." (Isaiah 6:8), but what depth and resonance they gain when we see them lived out by God the Son, Jesus Christ. Prior to his earthbound life, Jesus was the one through whom all of creation was made: not only this world that is our home, not only this solar system in which our world resides, but two trillion galaxies. Two trillion! Galaxies!!

He resided in glory—eternal, omnipresent, invulnerable to want or pain … until he left it all behind. From glory to a feeding trough, from eternity to the second-by-second passage of human time, from omnipresence to the confines of a finite human body, from invulnerable to vulnerable … to hunger, thirst, weakness, pain, and death. Why? To break the chains of sin and free us from eternal death, once for all (Romans 6:10). This was his mission. God the Son, Jesus Christ, gave one hundred percent, he was fully invested, he was all in … for us.

Oh, Holy God—We can't begin to imagine the glorious wonder of your heavenly home; we can't begin to comprehend the full depth, breadth, and scope of your all-powerful presence; and so we can't begin to properly appreciate all that you have done for us. All that you have given for us. From creator of all to servant of all, from exalted to condemned. Forgive us for too frequently taking this incomparable gift for granted. Forgive us for failing to reflect this outpouring of love in our attitudes, words, and actions. To you we give all thanks and all praise, now and forevermore. In the name of our precious savior, Jesus Christ, we pray. Amen.

5

IT'S PERSONAL

Jesus went through all the towns and villages, teaching in their synagogues, proclaiming the good news of the kingdom and healing every disease and sickness. When he saw the crowds, he had compassion on them, because they were harassed and helpless, like sheep without a shepherd.
—Matthew 9:35–36

During the years of Jesus' ministry, crowds flocked to hear him speak (Luke 5:1–3), throngs lined up for his healing touch (Matthew 15:30–31), people pressed on every side (Mark 5:21–31). Here he was, the God of all creation, in the thick of the desperate, jostling crowd, immersed in the churning sea of humanity.

What king—much less an all-powerful god—would do this? What king would walk away from his throne to mingle with the dirty, smelly, ignoble masses? God the Son, Jesus Christ, made this choice. To him, the people weren't a nuisance or a distraction, they weren't an intrusion or a hindrance. They were his mission: each and every one … welcomed, valued, loved. Loved enough to set aside all his riches and glory (compare with Luke 18:18–23); loved enough to die for. Because with God, it's personal.

Oh, King of Kings and Lord of Lords—"What is man that you are mindful of him?" That you, the one and only, all-powerful, everlasting God, would choose to become one of us, would choose to mix and mingle with us … It boggles the mind, and yet it's true. To this very day, you meet each one of us where we are … in the midst of doubt and fear, injury and illness, anger and sorrow, suffering and loss. In the midst of the messiness of life, you are our ever-present refuge and strength, joy and hope, savior, guide, and friend. Your love never fails. And for that, we give you thanks and praise. In the name of Jesus Christ, our Lord and Savior, we pray. Amen.

Verse cited in the prayer: Psalm 8:4, New King James Version.

6

BOTH-AND

A man with leprosy came and knelt before him and said, "Lord, if you are willing, you can make me clean." Jesus reached out his hand and touched the man. "I am willing," he said. "Be clean!"
—Matthew 8:2–3

"This is my blood of the covenant, which is poured out for many for the forgiveness of sins."
—Matthew 26:28

Either-or, neither-nor, both-and. Do you remember learning those pairs? She neither walked the dog nor fed the cat; she either walked the dog or fed the cat; she both walked the dog and fed the cat. Jesus came into a world full of both-ands: both physical and spiritual oppression, both physical and spiritual hurt, both physical and spiritual blindness, both physical and spiritual hunger and thirst. To this world of both-and need, God sent a both-and savior—fully God, fully man—who loved with a both-and love.

When vast crowds followed him, Jesus nourished their bodies with fish and bread, while nourishing their spirits with words of life (Luke 9:10–17). In Cana, he turned water into wine at a wedding banquet (John 2:1–11); and in Samaria, he offered living water to the woman at the well (John 4:1–42). To those who were blind, he gave sight (Luke 18:35–43); and through his teachings to the disciples, he gave the ability to truly see (Matthew 13:16). He raised Lazarus from the dead (John 11:43–44), and then he, himself, died on a cross and rose again, conquering sin and death once for all (Luke 23:44–46; Luke 24:5–7).

This, then, is God's "kingdom come": restoration of both body and soul. And this, then, is "thy will be done": meeting the need, both temporal and eternal. Because this is the only true kind of love: both-and.

Oh, Loving God—Our hearts overflow with gratitude and our spirits sing your praise. You give us both bread for today and the bread of life eternal. You give us both strength for the moment and hope everlasting. You meet every hurt, every struggle, every malady, every loss—whether of body or spirit—with tenderness and compassion, with transformative love. May we dedicate our lives to reflecting the both-and love that we have received. In the name of the one who is fully God and fully man, our Lord and Savior Jesus Christ, we pray. Amen.

7

I SURRENDER ALL

"My Father, if it is possible, may this cup be taken from me.
Yet not as I will, but as you will."
—Matthew 26:39

In your relationships with one another, have the same
mindset as Christ Jesus: Who, being in very nature God,
did not consider equality with God something to be used to
his own advantage; rather, he made himself nothing by taking the
very nature of a servant, being made in human likeness.
And being found in appearance as a man, he humbled
himself by becoming obedient to death —
even death on a cross!
—Philippians 2:5–8

According to ancient Jewish historian Josephus Flavius, in AD 70, following several years of ultimately unsuccessful rebellion against the Roman Empire, a band of roughly one thousand Jewish Zealots took refuge in Masada, a virtually impregnable fortress built by Herod the Great. In AD 73, the Romans lay siege to the fortress and, using a battering ram, broke through the walls. Once inside, they found only a handful of survivors; all others—including women, children, and the elderly—had been put to death by the Zealots, themselves. Why? Because the Zealots considered themselves to be servants of God alone, and therefore deemed it better to die than to succumb to Roman authority. (More information can be found at http://www.jewishvirtuallibrary.org/masada-desert-fortress, as well as other sites.)

Consider the stark contrast provided by Jesus of Nazareth. He was born inauspiciously in a stable in Bethlehem, thanks to a decree by Caesar Augustus (and obeyed by his parents) that a census of the Roman world be taken (Luke 2:1–7). And he died ignobly at the hands of Roman soldiers who nailed him to a Roman cross. This after being arrested by a Roman detachment (along with Jewish officials), tried by the Roman governor, taunted and flogged by Roman soldiers, and made to carry his own cross (John 18–19). For a Jewish man, there could not have been a more ignominious death. And what about for a man who was God? What about for One through whom all things had been made, and to whom these Roman authorities owed their very existence (John 1:1–3, 10)?

Jesus paid the ultimate price to secure eternal life for us. That we know. But our understanding of his sacrifice depends on the lens that we use. Did Jesus surrender to the Romans? Or to God the Father? Was his treatment at the hands of the Romans humiliating? Or was it an act of humble obedience and love? When is surrender a loss? And when is it a triumph? How we answer these questions creates two distinct paths: one that leads to Masada, and one that leads to the cross. What holds true, regardless, is that Jesus surrendered all … for us.

Oh God, our Father—We come before you overwhelmed by the incomparable gift of your son, Jesus Christ. Our hearts overflow with gratitude and praise for all that was done for us. He traded his exalted home on high for a life limited to the confines of human existence. He dedicated himself to meeting the needs of the people, both physical and spiritual, up to and including death on a cross so that we might have eternal life. Jesus paid it all—Jesus surrendered all—to you, for us. To him be all glory and praise. In the name of Jesus Christ, our Lord and Savior, we pray. Amen.

Devotion title drawn from "I Surrender All" by Judson W. Van DeVenter (1896). Public domain.

Notes

Who Does God Say that I Am?

8

WHO DOES GOD SAY THAT I AM?

The Lord does not look at the things people look at. People look at the outward appearance, but the Lord looks at the heart.
—1 Samuel 16:7

"Tell me about ya," the gentleman says, his countenance alight, his eyes full of good cheer, and his voice a marvelous Irish brogue. It's the greeting I've come to expect from this delightful acquaintance of several years, but this unforeseen encounter at the coffee shop means I'm not prepared. No easy "How have you been?" with its automatic, "Fine, how are you?" response. "Tell me about ya," he asks, knowing full well that it forces a more meaningful exchange. What to focus on? Work? Family? Something else? What I'm doing or how I'm feeling? What has already happened or what I hope for? The transient matters of the moment or the ongoing big picture?

Functioning within the framework of routine—in which certain tasks and interactions become rote—is perfectly normal, even helpful. But routine also has a way of, over time, constraining thought and creating blinders. For Christians, it can be oh-so-easy for our fundamental identities—who we are in God's eyes—to get tucked away in mental nooks as school and work and kids and parents and everything else piles up and over and around. And yet, that understanding of who we are affects everything: our priorities, our choices, our attitudes, our words, our actions.

So for the next few days, we'll try to dig past the routine and take a look at ourselves afresh, from God's perspective as conveyed in scripture. What do we have in common with all of humankind? In what ways are we different? And what difference does it make? What is our response to, "Tell me about ya'"?

Dear Father in Heaven—You have bestowed upon us not only the gift of salvation, but also the gift of identity. We confess that in the midst of the everyday hustle and bustle, that identify can get lost in the shuffle, and it sometimes gets a little tarnished, dented, and dinged. Help us to look at ourselves with new eyes … with your eyes. Help us to dig into who we are, who you meant for us to be, and to come away restored, renewed, and ready for service. In the name of our Lord and Savior, Jesus Christ, we pray. Amen.

9

WONDERFULLY MADE

I praise you because I am fearfully and wonderfully made...
—Psalm 139:14

Consider the human form. A universe of atoms with their sun-like nuclei and orbiting electrons clustered into bone-, sinew-, and organ-forming "galaxies," creating, out of the invisible (to the naked eye), the visible. Spiraling constellations of DNA, microscopic in size but wielding life-building power. Branching blood vessels carrying life-sustaining oxygen, nutrients, and warrior white blood cells in a rapid mass transit unrivaled by human endeavor. And a network of neurological sensors and triggers relaying information faster than a thought, a breath, or a heartbeat, and on which all three depend.

What a breathtaking convergence of art and science! A masterpiece pointing to the One in whom all art and science have their origin. And into this wondrous creation God breathes life—a soul formed in his image, made to align with his Spirit, intended to be as one with him. A mysterious conjoining of spirit and flesh; a promise of an eternal hope housed within a temporal vessel.

Breathtakingly beautiful. Incomprehensibly complex. Immeasurably precious. Unconditionally loved. Filled with hope and promise and potential. This is each of us. This is all of us.

Oh, God our Father—How wondrous are the works of your hands! Even the minutest details—invisible to the naked eye—are beautiful in form and awe-inspiring in function. How we revel in this creative display, and how we rejoice in the One who is its source! We confess that the spirit breathed into each of us with such love and hope is too frequently twisted out of alignment with you, too often reflects a distorted image. Please pour your forgiveness over us and make us anew. And may we, in turn, pour forth the blessing of your mercy, forgiveness, and grace upon others. In the name of our Lord and Savior, Jesus Christ, we pray. Amen.

10

LOST AND FOUND

There is no difference between Jew and Gentile, for all have sinned and fall short of the glory of God, and all are justified freely by his grace through the redemption that came by Christ Jesus.
—Romans 3:23–24

I head to the overflowing lost-and-found in search of a lost jacket. Hanging against the wall are sweatshirts, jackets, and vests, while hats, gloves, bottles, and lunchboxes are arrayed on a table. Among the jackets, I find some with hoods and some without, some that zip up and some that pull over, lightweight windbreakers and fleecy coats. Their individual characteristics notwithstanding, they share the same plight: they are unequivocally lost, separated from their owners, at least temporarily and sometimes permanently.

Similar to these lost garments, we, too, are prone to going astray, although in our case, it is by our own volition. Our individual circumstances notwithstanding—whether powerful or powerless, rich or poor, housed or homeless, highly educated or illiterate, upstanding citizen or convicted felon, teetotaler or addict—in and of ourselves, we share the same plight: we are unequivocally lost, separated from the One to whom we belong by a chasm that neither effort nor will can bridge. But Jesus is forever faithful. He seeks us out and brings us home (if we are willing), even at the cost of his own life.

Through Christ we were created, and through him we are redeemed. Before his cross, though no one is deserving, all are invited. And before his throne, none can claim to be self-made.

Our Father in Heaven—Left to our own devices, we are utterly lost. The divide between you and us is one that we cannot hope to bridge, no matter how we might try. But you love us so much that, no matter how lost we have become, no matter the distance from you that we have traveled, no matter how undeserving we are, you seek us out. And through your son, Jesus Christ, we are restored to you. Through Christ, alone, we are saved; through Christ, alone, we who were lost, are found. May we, as your followers, be willing to seek the hurting and the lost, and to extend restorative love to them, undiminished by condition or circumstance, just as you continually do for us. In the name of our Lord and Savior, Jesus Christ, we pray. Amen.

11

A CHILD OF ABRAHAM

Understand, then, that those who have faith are children of Abraham.
—Galatians 3:7

Studies have shown that children benefit from knowing their family history. Family stories create a connection across generations, providing children with a sense of identity that contributes to emotional well-being and resilience. We, too, have a shared family history, a lineage not of blood but of faith. What does our lineage tell us about who we are? What does it mean to be children of Abraham?

God said to Abram (not yet Abraham):

> "Go from your country, your people and your father's household to the land I will show you. I will make you into a great nation, and I will bless you; I will make your name great, and you will be a blessing. I will bless those who bless you, and whoever curses you I will curse; and all peoples on earth will be blessed through you" (Genesis 12:1–3).

Jesus said something similar to his disciples (a group that now includes us):

> "All authority in heaven and on earth has been given to me. Therefore go and make disciples of all nations, baptizing them in the name of the Father and of the Son and of the Holy Spirit, and teaching them to obey everything I have commanded you. And surely I am with you always, to the very end of the age" (Matthew 28:19–20).

So what does our family history tell us about who we are? We are made to go: go wherever God's will takes us. We are made to be nation-builders (a.k.a. kingdom-builders): we will have spiritual descendants as numerous as the stars (see Genesis 15:5). We are made to bless: through us, all people of every nation will be blessed, "for we are God's handiwork, created in Christ Jesus to do good works, which God prepared in advance for us to do" (Ephesians 2:10). And God's got our back: come what may, God is with us, and "if God is for us, who can be against us?" (Romans 8:31). We are, indeed, blessed.

Oh, Mighty God, Our Father—How grateful we are to have been adopted into the lineage of Abraham! What a blessing it is to be heirs to the blessing that was first given to him. We pray that you will embed our lineage into our hearts and minds so that we will better understand who we are called to be, and so that we will courageously carry out all that we are called to do. In the name of our Lord and Savior, Jesus Christ, we pray. Amen.

12

HIS AMBASSADOR

We are therefore Christ's ambassadors, as though God were making his appeal through us.
—2 Corinthians 5:20

We play many roles. We are sons, daughters, sisters, brothers, mothers, fathers, husbands, wives, friends, neighbors, workers, managers, teachers, coaches, students, and so on. No matter how long or short the list, there is one role that takes primacy, by far, over all the rest: we are, first and foremost, ambassadors for Jesus Christ and his kingdom.

What is an ambassador? In short, ambassadors are appointed by the leader of their home country to live and work in a foreign country where, through their words and actions, they represent the interests and policies of their home country.

We, then, have been appointed by Jesus Christ, the one who has been given "all authority in heaven and on earth" (Mt. 28:18), to live and work in a foreign land (this world; Jn. 17:16–18), where we represent the interests (reconciliation; 2 Cor. 5:18–19) and policies (to love; Mt. 22:37–39) of our eternal, heavenly home (Phil. 3:18–20). We do so through our words (the gospel message; Mk. 16:15) and our actions, as set out by God: eliminating injustice, slavery, and oppression; feeding the hungry; providing shelter and clothing to those in need; caring for the sick; and visiting the incarcerated (Is. 58:6–7; Mt. 25:35–36). In short, by caring for those who are most vulnerable, overlooked, and ostracized.

As followers of Christ, this is what we are appointed to do, what we were created to do (Eph. 2:10). The only question for us is this: do we accept the assignment?

Almighty God, Our Father—We confess that we get too easily caught up in the roles of this earth, until they become the core of who we are and what we do. We too easily forget, or set aside, your higher call to be your ambassador; a call that, to be fully carried out, requires our constant awareness, constant dedication, constant communication with you. Instill in our hearts a desire to be fully representative of you, in every thought, attitude, word, and action. Draw us ever closer to you, so that in all that we are and do, people see not us, but you. In the name of our Lord and Savior, Jesus Christ, we pray. Amen.

13

INTEGRAL TO HIS PLAN

Now you are the body of Christ, and each
one of you is a part of it.
—1 Corinthians 12:27

God has placed the parts in the body, every
one of them, just as he wanted them to be.
—1 Corinthians 12:18

"Why are you here?" Imagine being met with that question upon entering a church. Or upon turning to fellow worshipers during a time of greeting. It wouldn't seem like much of a warm welcome. And yet … why are you here? And why am I here? How did we choose to become part of a particular church, a particular collection of God's people?

Perhaps the location is convenient. Or it has good programs for children and youth. Or it offers an appealing worship style. Or we like the Bible study options. Or the people are friendly and welcoming. Or any number of other perfectly good reasons to choose a church, which is how we tend to think of it, right? We assess the options and choose a church, one that seems well-suited to us: our convictions, interests, and needs.

But what if that's not quite right? What if that's not the whole picture? What if, as we're choosing, God is leading, guiding us in a particular direction, drawing us to where we're meant to be? What if the reason why we're here comes not from us, but from God?

Because the truth is, he has a purpose for you, and for me. And he takes his purpose for you and he weaves it together with his purpose for me. And then he weaves us together with the older gentleman who sits up front where he can hear better, and with the young girl who's on the edge of her seat waiting for the children's story, and with the woman who slips in a little late and slips out a little early. And he continues his weaving until his purpose for each of us melds into a plan for all of us, together. Until we become one fabric, one body, one church. A church created by him, specially designed by him to respond to his call and carry out his will. A church well-suited to him.

Dear Father God—Why are we here? Why am I here? We confess that, as prone as we are to ask these questions in relation to life, we too frequently fail to ask them in relation to the church. And yet, you have a purpose for each of us within the church; individual purposes that you bind into a plan for all of us, together. A plan that enables us to do more, to become more, than we ever could alone. Open our hearts and minds to all that you would have us be and do, open our eyes to the opportunities placed before us. In the name of our Lord and Savior, Jesus Christ, we pray. Amen.

Notes

So What?

14

SO WHAT?

"Follow me, and I will make you fishers of men."
—Matthew 4:19

We've considered, by focusing on the missions example provided by God, himself: the willingness of God the Son, Jesus Christ, to go from ruler of all to servant of all, on our behalf; his direct, personal engagement with, and love for, the people; his dedication to meeting both physical (temporal) and spiritual (eternal) needs; and his complete surrender to God the Father's will, no matter the cost.

We then focused on who we are in God's eyes. As humans, each and every one of us is a precious creation, beautifully and wonderfully made, but each and every one of us is also unequivocally, hopelessly lost without the wholly undeserved intervention of Jesus Christ. As Christians, we are, by faith, children of Abraham, made to be a blessing to all the world and to be actively involved in building God's kingdom. We are also God's ambassadors, appointed to be fully representative of him in all that we say and do. And we are, every single one of us, an integral part of his plan, a plan that relies on our working together as one church to carry out the mission that he places before us.

So what? What difference does this make in our lives? This topic will be our focus for the next few days.

Almighty God—What great lengths you have gone to for us! You inspire our worship, gratitude, and praise. What's more, you invite us to join you in your mission, to work hand-in-glove with you to build your kingdom. What an unparalleled blessing! But the truth is that, when viewed clearly and unshirkingly, the example you've given us is a daunting one. How can we possibly live up to it? How can we possibly represent you fully and accurately in all that we say and do? And yet, though you know us perfectly, every limitation and frailty, your commitment to us—to working with us and through us, as conduits of your blessing—never wavers. You call to us persistently and unceasingly, drawing us ever closer to you, and into the world for you. Teach us to place our confidence not in what we can do, but in what you can do in and through us. Teach us not to believe in ourselves, but to believe in you in us. In the name of our Lord and Savior, Jesus Christ, we pray. Amen.

15

LIVING LARGE

For even the Son of Man did not come to be served, but to serve, and to give his life as a ransom for many
—Mark 10:45

Back in the '90s, the phrase "living large" was trending. It connoted success, wealth, extravagance. It was all about having the best stuff, and lots of it. More recently, "YOLO" picked up where "living large" left off, with a focus on acquiring experiences rather than stuff, because You Only Live Once. Despite the slight difference, the two share the same orientation: a focus on oneself, the paradoxical consequence being that every attempt to live the largest possible life produces the smallest possible life.

What, then, is the secret to the largest possible life? It isn't a secret at all: "Love the Lord your God with all your heart and with all your soul and with all your mind" (Matthew 22:37).

From this root, the rest bursts forth: "Love your neighbor as yourself" (Matthew 22:38), "love your enemies and pray for those who persecute you" (Matthew 5:44), "spend yourselves in behalf of the hungry and satisfy the needs of the oppressed" (Isaiah 58:10).

A life focused on ourselves imprisons us within the blip of time between birth and death, and confines us to the geographical pinpoints of our physical locations. But a life so drenched in God's love that it spills outward, pouring into the lives of not only family and friends but also mere acquaintances, total strangers, and even enemies, reverberates across time and space. Such a life reaches out in love to those both near and far. Such a life transforms not only the here and now, but all eternity.

What does such a life look like? God, himself, provides the answer:

> "Is not this the kind of fasting I [God] have chosen: to loose the chains of injustice and untie the cords of the yoke, to set the oppressed free and break every yoke? Is it not to share your food with the hungry and to provide the poor wanderer with shelter—when you see the naked, to clothe them, and not to turn away from your own flesh and blood?" (Isaiah 58:6–7).

And, again:

> "Then the King will say to those on his right, 'Come, you who are blessed by my Father; take your inheritance, the kingdom prepared for you since the creation of the world. For I was hungry and you gave me something to eat, I was thirsty and you gave me something to drink, I was a stranger and you invited me in, I needed clothes and you clothed me, I was sick and you looked after me, I was in prison and you came to visit me'" (Matthew 25:34–36).

We are all given the choice: to live small or to live truly large. So why not live large? Because, you know, YOLO.

Dear Heavenly Father—We thank you for the opportunity you give us to live truly large, to live a life unbound by the confines of geography and time. Instill within us your love: a love that can never be satisfied with the status quo, a love that can never be content with doing nothing, a love that both accepts and transforms, a love that is unstoppable in its power and bottomless in its depth. In the name of our Lord and Savior, Jesus Christ, we pray. Amen.

Notes

16

EVERYDAY TRANSCENDENCE

Your kingdom come.
—Matthew 6:10

So we fix our eyes not on what is seen, but on what is unseen, since what is seen is temporary, but what is unseen is eternal.
—2 Corinthians 4:18

Have you ever reached for binoculars to better see something in the distance, only to become disoriented because the focus (still in place from a prior use) was all off? Or have you picked up the wrong pair of glasses—reading glasses when distance vision was needed, or vice versa—thereby blinding yourself to what you needed to see while gaining a crystal clear view of what you didn't need to see?

God offers us a similar choice: to see through the lens of this world or through the lens of his Spirit. The choice we make has no effect on what is present, but creates a seismic shift in what we see. One lens confines us to the here and now, while the other opens up eternity; one fetters us to the mundane, while the other reveals the burgeoning presence of God's kingdom; and one tends to focus on things to be done, while the other focuses on people encountered along the way.

People like the busker on the street corner, who day in and day out, trumpets out hymns that can be heard down the block. And like the charming man standing outside the bakery, whose cheerful smile and appeal for a warm cup of coffee are impossible to resist. People like the hard-working cashier at the local pharmacy, who was recently diagnosed with cancer, and the homeless veteran who stands at the intersection, requesting spare change while people are stopped at the traffic light.

People like the gregarious hawker of Street Sense, a newspaper by the homeless for the homeless. He's quick to offer a copy of a poem he wrote, a source of personal pride because it elicited a letter from the then president of the United States (which he'll also happily share). It's such a small thing … a letter. How many are sent out over the course of a presidential term? But of all those letters, this one was meant specifically for him, and that is no small thing.

That's how God works, too, isn't it? Through seemingly small things that, after all, aren't so small. Through kind words spoken, smiles exchanged, a shoulder to cry on, a helping hand, a cup of coffee, a meal provided, a lift to the store or doctor's office, help with schoolwork or a job application, and so much more. In God's hands, small kindnesses reveal his kingdom and small acts of compassion reverberate across eternity. In God's hands, the everyday becomes transcendent.

Do you see the kingdom of God? Will you be the kingdom of God? Will you be God's personal letter to the overlooked people of this world?

Father God—Send your Spirit to us, so that we may truly see. Give us eyes that see with compassion, ears that hear more than just what's spoken, and hands that are willing to serve. Most of all, give us hearts that are ready to love. In the name of our Lord and Savior, Jesus Christ, we pray. Amen.

Notes

17

SPEND YOURSELVES

And if you spend yourselves in behalf of the hungry and satisfy the needs of the oppressed, then your light will rise in the darkness, and your night will become like the noonday.
—Isaiah 58:10

What does it mean to spend yourself? We spend time and money, but how can I spend myself? What does "myself" comprise? Certainly, the knowledge I have gleaned over time, the wisdom I have gained from experience, the skills I have acquired through training and practice, the God-given talents I was born with and have nurtured, and the spiritual gifts that God bestows in his perfect timing. In addition to these are my energy, my time, my attention, my personal connections, and whatever resources I have at my disposal. In short, God is saying that all that I am is to be brought to bear in behalf of the hungry and oppressed; not only brought to bear, but fully devoted to the cause.

But who are these hungry and oppressed people, for whom I'm called to spend myself? They are the breathtakingly beautiful, immeasurably precious people (see Day 9) who have become overlooked and ostracized, forgotten and lost. They are those afflicted with pain and injury, addiction and illness. They are the abused and those held captive. They are the incarcerated and the despised.

In short, they are us, in the absence of Christ's mercy and saving grace: addicted to the things of this world; imprisoned within the walls of our own self-absorption, and bound fast by chains of sin forged by our own hands; terminally ill and utterly lost to God (see Day 10).

Seeing our condition, Jesus gave all, surrendered all, for us (see Days 4 and 7). Will we, then, who claim to be his followers, who call him Lord, not do the same (Matthew 7:21)?

> "For even the Son of Man did not come to be served, but to serve, and to give his life as a ransom for many" (Mark 10:45).
>
> "Whoever wants to be my disciple must deny themselves and take up their cross daily and follow me. For whoever wants to save their life will lose it, but whoever loses their life for me will save it" (Luke 9:23–24).

Yet this is not a call to sacrifice, but a call to surrender. For if all that we are and have belongs to God, then where is the loss? And if all that we treasure resides with him, then where is the sacrifice?

We are called to love with the both-and love of our Lord and Savior, Jesus Christ (see Day 6); we are called to be a blessing to all nations, to be kingdom-builders (see Day 11); we are called to be all in, fully invested, not out of duty or obligation, but out of love, because when anyone is hurting, it's personal (see Days 4 and 5).

Let us, like Paul, declare by word and deed, "For to me, to live is Christ and to die is gain" (Philippians 1:21).

Oh, Merciful God—We confess that surrender is not easy. Although we well know of Christ's complete surrender on our behalf, yet we cling to the attitudes, viewpoints, and things of this world. We plead with you to draw us close, so that no option but surrender remains. May our hearts, spirits, and lives sing out, "break my heart for what breaks yours, everything I am for your kingdom's cause" and "I surrender all," because "love so amazing, so divine, demands my soul, my life, my all." In the name of our Lord and Savior, Jesus Christ, we pray. Amen.

Songs cited, in order of mention: "Hosanna" by Brooke Fraser, ©2006 Hillsong Publishing; "I Surrender All" by Judson W. Van DeVenter (1896; public domain); "When I Survey the Wondrous Cross" by Isaac Watts (1707; public domain).

Notes____

18

COME TOGETHER, RIGHT NOW, OVER ME

I have given them the glory that you gave me, that they may be one as we are one—I in them and you in me—so that they may be brought to complete unity.
—John 17:22

And let us consider how we may spur one another on toward love and good deeds, not giving up meeting together, as some are in the habit of doing, but encouraging one another.
—Hebrews 10:24–25

"This little light of mine, I'm gonna let it shine. This little light of mine, I'm gonna let it shine." Who remembers singing that as a child? How I remember our fierce determination as we sang, "Won't let Satan [blowing sound] it out, I'm gonna let it shine!"

It's a wonderful reminder of Jesus' words: "You are the light of the world … let your light shine before others, that they may see your good deeds and glorify your Father in heaven" (Matthew 5:14, 16). The only problem is that the childhood imagery can be limiting: a vision of flickering candles sprinkled here and there amidst a vast darkness; this "little" light.

Candlelight services take us a step further, giving us a sense of our collective light as the darkness gradually yields to each newly lit candle. Yet shadowy nooks and rafters inevitably remain. And as beautiful and meaningful as the imagery is, it belies the darkness-shattering power that God, himself, has promised to us, his collective people, his Church:

> "If you do away with the yoke of oppression, with the pointing finger and malicious talk, and if you spend yourselves in behalf of the hungry and satisfy the needs of the oppressed, then your light will rise in the darkness, and your night will become like the noonday" (Isaiah 58:9–10).

Like the noonday! Forget about candles. When we, together, work to meet physical and spiritual needs, night becomes noonday! No darkness, no shadows; all light.

Over the next few days, we'll look at a selection of God's promises to his people, his Church; big, bold, life-altering, world-altering promises that hinge on one thing: being all in, together. Let's turn on the light!

Almighty God—We thank you for your Church, a gift not only to the world, but also to us, your children. Together, we do more and become more than we ever could alone. Made one by your Spirit, and committed to applying our collective knowledge, skills, talents, gifts, and passions to your work, a new reality unfolds that, otherwise, would never be revealed. We pray that you will instill your Spirit within us, binding us together as one, so that we, with all the world, will see your promises fulfilled. In the name of our Lord and Savior, Jesus Christ, we pray. Amen.

Devotion title drawn from "Come Together" (1969), written by John Lennon and Paul McCartney. ©EMI Music Publishing, Sony/ATV Music Publishing LLC.Song cited in the devotion: "This Little Light of Mine" by Harry Dixon Loes. Public domain.

Notes

God's Promises

19

GOD WITH US (PART 1)

Is not this the kind of fasting I [God] have chosen: to loose the chains of injustice and untie the cords of the yoke, to set the oppressed free and break every yoke? Is it not to share your food with the hungry and to provide the poor wanderer with shelter—when you see the naked, to clothe them, and not to turn away from your own flesh and blood? Then your light will break forth like the dawn, and your healing will quickly appear; then your righteousness will go before you, and the glory of the Lord will be your rear guard. Then you will call, and the Lord will answer; you will cry for help, and he will say: Here am I.
—Isaiah 58:6–9

When the Israelites arrived at the land of Canaan following their liberation from Egypt, Moses sent out scouts to explore the land. The scouts returned with reports of a land flowing with milk and honey … and also already claimed by a powerful people (like giants, to the scouts) with large, fortified cities. God had faithfully led the Israelites to this place, this Promised Land; he had prepared them for this very moment; but when faced with a land of giants, they chose, not God's path, but their own. A path that led them straight back into the desert for another 40 years (Numbers 13 and 14).

When a new generation of Israelites later returned to Canaan, they faced the same adversity, but they accepted God's call and trusted his leadership. With priests carrying the ark of the covenant and sounding trumpets, the Israelites marched around the city of Jericho. On the seventh day, after seven times around the city, the army gave a loud shout, and the walls of Jericho fell, allowing the Israelites to race in and capture the city. God had delivered the city into their hands (Joshua 6).

Today, God calls us, his people, into a world equally full of promise, a world flowing with milk and honey. But it is also a world wrapped in darkness and bound by sin. It is overrun by the giants of poverty, fear, hunger, violence, greed, and hatred, to name only a few. God calls us to lay claim to this land. He calls each collection of his followers (each church) to a territory of his choosing: a place to which he has been faithfully leading us all along, and a battle for which he has fully prepared us; a place where we are meant to be a blessing, and to be blessed. But like the Israelites, we must choose, individually and collectively, whether to follow God's call … or not.

Those who decline his invitation find themselves wandering in a desert of their own making. But those who accept God's invitation are recipients of God's promise to Joshua:

> "Be strong and courageous. Do not be afraid; do not be discouraged, for the Lord your God will be with you wherever you go" (Joshua 1:9).

And of his promise to his people through Isaiah:

> "Then your righteousness will go before you, and the glory of the Lord will be your rear guard. Then you will call, and the Lord will answer; you will cry for help, and he will say: Here am I" (Isaiah 58:8–9)

But what is our righteousness? And how does it go before us? We'll dive into these questions next.

Oh, God, Our Steadfast Guardian and Guide—If you are for us, who can be against us? Before you, fortified walls crumble and giants are vanquished. Darkness flees from your presence. You declare to your enemies, "Be still, and know that I am God." You are our refuge and strength. You are our fortress and our deliverer. You are Immanuel (God with us). "Therefore, we will praise you, Lord, among nations; we will sing praises of your name." In the name of our Lord and Savior, Jesus Christ, we pray. Amen.

Verses cited in the prayer: Romans 8:31; Psalm 46:1, 10; and Psalm 18:2, 49.

Notes

20

GOD WITH US (PART 2)

*Is not this the kind of fasting I [God] have chosen: to loose the chains of injustice and untie the cords of the yoke, to set the oppressed free and break every yoke? Is it not to share your food with the hungry and to provide the poor wanderer with shelter—when you see the naked, to clothe them, and not to turn away from your own flesh and blood? ...**Then your righteousness will go before you, and the glory of the Lord will be your rear guard.***
—Isaiah 58:6–8, emphasis added

Yesterday we considered how, like the Israelites as they laid claim to the Promised Land, we too are called by God into a land of giants—poverty, fear, hunger, violence, greed, and hatred—to lay claim to it; to be a blessing and to be blessed. To those who heed his call, God promises his presence. In particular, in Isaiah 58:8, God promises, "then your righteousness will go before you, and the glory of the Lord will be your rear guard."

But what is our righteousness?

Perhaps it is the act of fighting injustice and oppression, hunger, poverty, and need. By doing so, we shine the light of love into the darkness around us, and we become known in our communities for the good that we do. With time, our reputation precedes us, overcoming obstacles that would have previously blocked our paths, drawing into the effort ever more people and resources, touching and transforming the lives of more and more people, all to God's glory ("and the glory of the Lord will be your rear guard"). Is this, then, our righteousness? Or is there more?

Why do we help the poor and the oppressed, the hungry and the vulnerable, the overlooked and the ostracized? Because our hearts, aligned with God's, mourn the suffering and brokenness, and desire healing and wholeness; because our minds, aligned with his, see beyond the ugliness of what is, to the beauty of what could be; and because our spirits, aligned with his, resolve to act, compelling us forward, unwilling to do nothing in the face of suffering, unwilling to accept the status quo. And so, aligned with God in heart, mind, and spirit, we can't help but align with him in action (strength), bringing healing to a broken world. ("Jesus replied: 'Love the Lord your God with all your heart and with all your soul and with all your mind.' This is the first and greatest commandment. And the second is like it: 'Love your neighbor as yourself'" Matthew 22:37–39.) Is this, then, our righteousness? Or is there more?

How is it that our hearts, minds, and spirits, and thereby our actions, become aligned with God's? It is through the one whose righteousness is credited to us, through faith, and through the intervention of his Spirit.

> "For just as through the disobedience of the one man the many were made sinners, so also through the obedience of the one man the many will be made righteous" (Romans 5:19).

> "But now apart from the law the righteousness of God has been made known, to which the Law and the Prophets testify. This righteousness is given through faith in Jesus Christ to all who believe" (Romans 3:21–22).

> "It is because of him that you are in Christ Jesus, who has become for us wisdom from God—that is, our righteousness, holiness and redemption" (1 Corinthians 1:30).

> "You heavens above, rain down my [God's] righteousness; let the clouds shower it down. Let the earth open wide, let salvation spring up, let righteousness flourish with it; I, the Lord, have created it" (Isaiah 45:8).

> "For through the Spirit we eagerly await by faith the righteousness for which we hope" (Galatians 5:5).

So what is our righteousness? Let's instead ask, who is our righteousness? Christ, himself, goes before us, the author of our righteousness; the one who aligns our hearts, minds, and spirits with his; the one who transforms us so that, through us, all the world may be transformed; the one whose glory is then revealed for all to see.

This, then, is God's promise to his people when we, together, heed his call: Christ, our Lord, before us and behind us, beginning and end, alpha and omega.

What are the practical implications? That is our next topic.

Oh, Holy and Righteous God—It is through you, through the gift of your son, Jesus Christ, that we are made righteous. In all that we are and do, it is not us but your son, going before us, coming behind us, living through us. Indeed, it is not we who live, but Christ who lives in us. We can therefore say with confidence that, truly, the Lord is near. And so we rejoice! Because with God, all things are possible. In praise of your holy name, and in the name of our Lord and Savior, Jesus Christ, we pray. Amen.

Verses cited in the prayer: Galatians 2:20; Philippians 4:4-5; and Mark 10:27

21

GOD WITH US (PART 3)

Is not this the kind of fasting I [God] have chosen: to loose the chains of injustice and untie the cords of the yoke, to set the oppressed free and break every yoke? Is it not to share your food with the hungry and to provide the poor wanderer with shelter—when you see the naked, to clothe them, and not to turn away from your own flesh and blood? ... ***Then your righteousness will go before you, and the glory of the Lord will be your rear guard.***
—Isaiah 58:6–8, emphasis added

God calls each collection of his people—each church—to a Promised Land of his choosing: a particular place, a particular group of people, a particular area of brokenness. To churches who heed his call, he promises his enveloping presence (see Days 19 and 20).

Why does this matter? What tangible, practical difference does it make?

In Isaiah 58:8, God uses a military analogy, so let's start there. "Then your righteousness will go before you"; i.e., an advance guard. The Department of Defense *Dictionary of Military and Associated Terms* describes an advance guard as follows:

> Detachment sent ahead of the main force to ensure its uninterrupted advance; to protect the main body against surprise; to facilitate the advance by removing obstacles and repairing roads and bridges; and to cover the deployment of the main body if it is committed to action.

How might this description be rewritten in relation to a church carrying out God's mission?

> Our righteousness, being Christ, himself, sent ahead of the main force, his people,
>
> - to ensure their uninterrupted (unstoppable) advance into the territory to which he has called them;
> - to protect his people against surprise attack by the forces of evil;

- to facilitate their advance by (a) removing obstacles—both tangible, logistical obstacles within this physical realm, and intangible obstacles thrown up within the spiritual realm—from their path, and by (b) laying the needed groundwork—drawing in the needed people and resources, and preparing hearts and minds and spirits;
- to provide protection to his people when they are committed to action through a convergence of God's will (call) and their own willingness (response).

Wow! We want this, right? What happens, though, if we choose to follow God's general call but not his specific call? For example, what if he calls us to reach out to the immigrant community, but we instead focus our efforts on those struggling with addiction? Both communities of people are dear to God, both goals are commendable. But consider the military: what happens if the main military body chooses a different path from that of its advance guard? It is now blazing its own path; it loses all of the preparation—the groundwork laid and the obstacles removed—and the protection of the advance guard. The promise is lost.

Similarly, what happens if we accept God's call, but with adjustments because the original vision seems, from our perspective, too daunting, impractical, or unsustainable? What if we modify it to suit our vision of what we think will work, will be achievable? It would be as if the military body never took more than a few steps beyond its existing fortifications. Of what use, then, is all of the preparation and protection of the advance guard? None at all; because it's never put to use. Here, too, the promise is lost, because we never step out into it, just as the Israelites under Moses failed to enter the Promised Land. The blessing that could have been given is not received; the victory that could have been claimed is not achieved; the glory that could have been revealed remains hidden.

Which brings us to the last portion of the verse: "the glory of the Lord will be your rear guard." The Department of Defense *Dictionary of Military and Associated Terms* describes the rear guard as follows:

1. The rearmost elements of an advancing or withdrawing force. It has the following functions: to protect the rear of a column from hostile forces; during withdrawal, to delay the enemy; during the advance, to keep supply routes open.

2. Security detachment that a moving ground force details to the rear to keep it informed and covered.

A church responding to God's call is a church that is advancing. Through our advance, God's glory is revealed—as when Joshua and the Israelites marched into and across the Promised Land—and forms our rear guard, providing protection from the forces of evil, replenishing us with the strength and renewal of God's Spirit, and supplying us with wisdom and discernment.

But, again, what happens if we go off-path or scale back the path to which we're called? Then God's glory remains hidden, the rear guard never comes into play, and the promise is lost.

Let us, then, be committed to action. And not just to any action, but the specific action—in full and without compromise—to which God calls us. Let us, like Joshua, be strong and courageous (Joshua 1:9), following our advance guard with unwavering confidence, and placing complete trust in the protection of our rear guard, so that God's promise will be ours in full.

[We can] remain confident of this: [we] will see the goodness of the Lord in the land of the living. Wait for the Lord; be strong and take heart and wait for the Lord (Psalm 27:13–14).

Lord, Our God—You are our light and our salvation—whom shall we fear? You are the stronghold of our lives—of whom shall we be afraid? You go before us, taking possession of the territory that you claim as your own. You go before us and you are with us; you will never leave us nor forsake us. Like the Psalmist we sing, "The Lord Almighty is with us; the God of Jacob is our fortress." Praise be to God! In the name of our Lord and Savior, Jesus Christ, we pray. Amen.

Verses cited in the prayer: Psalm 27:1; Deuteronomy 31:1-8; and Psalm 46:11.

Notes____

22

RETURN TO THE GARDEN

If you do away with the yoke of oppression, with the pointing finger and malicious talk, and if you spend yourselves in behalf of the hungry and satisfy the needs of the oppressed, then your light will rise in the darkness, and your night will become like the noonday... ***You will be like a well-watered garden, like a spring whose waters never fail.***
—Isaiah 58:9–11, emphasis added

What comes to mind when you think of a well-watered garden? Sun-dappled trees with birdsong rising from within lush foliage? Vibrant cascades of flowers, luring busy bees and dancing butterflies to their showy display? Dense bushes laden with succulent berries, ripe for the picking?

What about that most iconic garden of all? The Garden of Eden.

Eden was a place of abundant life. Fed by a spring (it seems) whose waters formed a river that wound through the garden and beyond, Eden was filled with trees and plants that were both beautiful to behold and provided food to eat (Genesis 2:9–10). In Eden, Adam and Eve's lives were filled with purpose, as they tended the garden in accordance with God's instruction; and with peace, as they lived in harmony with one another, with the world in which they resided, and with God (Genesis 2:15, 25).

In the promise of Isaiah 58:11, the Garden of Eden becomes not a place, but a state of being, capable of existing anywhere. As our hearts, minds, and spirits become aligned with God's, and as we work together, as a church, to carry out his will (Isaiah 58:9–10), we are filled with life and purpose; we are nourished by his Spirit; and we are at peace with ourselves, with one another, and with God. We become Eden. Wherever we gather together, the garden is there, too. When we venture into the world, doing God's work, we bring the garden with us.

This is God's promise to us, his church. A return to harmony. A return to abundant life. A return to Eden.

Dear God, Our Creator and Author of All Life—How we long for a return to Eden. How we yearn to see your garden restored. We beseech you to draw us ever closer to you—heart, mind, soul, and strength, to draw us ever more into your will, so that we might see your promise revealed. So that we will be your promise fulfilled. In the name of our Lord and Savior, Jesus Christ, we pray. Amen.

23

A NEW JERUSALEM

If you do away with the yoke of oppression, with the pointing finger and malicious talk, and if you spend yourselves in behalf of the hungry and satisfy the needs of the oppressed, then your light will rise in the darkness, and your night will become like the noonday... You will be like a well-watered garden, like a spring whose waters never fail. ***Your people will rebuild the ancient ruins and will raise up the age-old foundations; you will be called Repairer of Broken Walls, Restorer of Streets with Dwellings.***

—Isaiah 58:9–12, emphasis added

What comes to mind when you think of ancient ruins? Cobblestone streets, once teaming with cacophonous life, now overtaken by rustling grasses or time's accumulated dust? Crumbling walls and piled rubble, the only evidence of homes where once children were born, guests were welcomed, the ill were tended, tears were dried, rest was found, and laughter spilled from doorways and windows?

What would it mean to rebuild such ancient ruins? What would be the significance of restoring such walls and streets and homes?

Let's look to Nehemiah for inspiration. His story begins in 446 BC, 140 years after the destruction of Jerusalem and the exile of the Jewish people to Babylon in 586 BC. By this time, Babylon had, itself, fallen to the Medes and the Persians (539 BC), and under their new rulers, the Jewish people had been permitted to return to Jerusalem, should they so choose. One group returned to Jerusalem in 538 BC, another group in 458 BC, and a third group returns with Nehemiah.

When we meet Nehemiah, he is living in Susa (the capital of Persia), where he is serving as the king's cupbearer, and he has just heard news from Judah: "They said to me, 'Those who survived the exile and are back in the province are in great trouble and disgrace. The wall of Jerusalem is broken down, and its gates have been burned with fire'" (Neh. 1:3). We also know, from later in the story (Neh. 7:4), that the homes in Jerusalem had been destroyed.

Why are these circumstances a source of great trouble? Without walls and gates, the city affords no protection to the people, even if there were homes to live in, which there aren't. The city is uninhabitable. And why are these circumstances a source of disgrace? For the Jewish people, the destroyed city is a reminder of their shame; their failure to obey God's commands (see Neh. 1:6–7). Even worse, what does such a shell of a city say about their God to the rest of the world?

It's no wonder that Nehemiah is filled with distress: "When I heard these things, I sat down and wept. For some days I mourned and fasted and prayed before the God of heaven" (Neh. 1:4). After mourning and praying, Nehemiah approaches the king with a request to go to Jerusalem to rebuild the city (Neh. 2:5). The king not only grants his request but also assists him in the endeavor (Neh. 2:7–9).

The rest of the story in a nutshell: Through an enormous, coordinated effort, the people rebuild the city walls, even while simultaneously guarding the city against attack from their none-too-pleased neighbors (Neh. 3–4, 6). Upon completion of the walls, the people gather to hear Ezra read from the Book of the Law of Moses and to receive instruction in the Law from the Levites. Worship is, thus, restored (Neh. 8–10). Nehemiah then repopulates the city, selecting the leaders of the people, plus one out of every ten from among the rest, to settle in Jerusalem (Neh. 11). And when everything is done, the wall is dedicated, with worship and celebration: "And on that day they offered great sacrifices, rejoicing because God had given them great joy. The women and children also rejoiced. The sound of rejoicing in Jerusalem could be heard far away" (Neh. 12:43).

So what does it mean when ancient ruins are restored? It means a renewal of relationships, with one another and with God; it means replacing mourning with joy; it means a transformation from desolation to abundant life; and it means that God is glorified.

What lies in ruins today? What do these ruins say about us, God's people? What do these ruins say about our God to the world around us? Do these ruins make us weep? Do we mourn and pray before God? Are we committed to rebuilding the ruins? Are we committed to working together—drawing on our collective knowledge, skills, talents, and passions—to accomplish the task?

If we "do away with the yoke of oppression, with the pointing finger and malicious talk,"
And if we "spend [our]selves in behalf of the hungry and satisfy the needs of the oppressed," …
Then we "will rebuild the ancient ruins and will raise up the age-old foundations; [we] will be called Repairer of Broken Walls, Restorer of Streets with Dwellings."

What does it mean when ancient ruins are restored? It means a new Jerusalem…a Jerusalem built not out of stone or clay, but out of our lives, bound one to another, with Christ as the cornerstone. This is God's promise.

Almighty God—We confess that we are mired in ruins … ruins that we too often prefer to ignore or justify or leave to others (or you) to sort out. Don't let us be content with doing so. Reveal to us the ruins in their full magnitude, so that we can't claim ignorance, and instill within us an unquenchable desire for, and an unwavering commitment to, their restoration. We long for a new Jerusalem. Help us to long for it enough to do something about it. In the name of our Lord and Savior, Jesus Christ, we pray. Amen.

Historical background drawn from various online resources, including http://www.biblereferenceguide.com/keywords/israel-return.html and https://biblicalstudies.org.uk/article_exile.html. Precise dates vary across sources.

Notes____

Mission Traps

24

MISSION TRAPS

Watch and pray so that you will not fall into temptation.
The spirit is willing, but the flesh is weak.
—Matthew 26:41

We began this series of devotions by looking at God's example of what being on mission means and by exploring who we are in God's eyes. Drawing on those insights, we then contemplated the question, so what? What difference does it make in our lives? From there, we moved on to study a few of God's extraordinary promises to his people, promises that come to fruition when we (his people, his Church) work together to carry out his will.

Now that we're excited to be a part of God's life-saving, kingdom-building mission—a call that's not just about a single moment in time or a single activity, but that permeates every day and every aspect of our lives—it's time to look at a few of the things that can trip us up along the way. We'll call them "mission traps."

When responding to God's call on our lives and dedicating ourselves to his mission, it can be easy, in our excitement, to overlook the temptations, or diversions, that could draw us off course. But the truth is, we remain human. And on top of that, when we commit to actively being a part of God's work, we become higher-profile targets in the eyes of the one whose goal it is to thwart God's efforts. Let there be no doubt, "our struggle is not against flesh and blood, but against the rulers, against the authorities, against the powers of this dark world and against the spiritual forces of evil in the heavenly realms" (Ephesians 6:12).

We can rest assured, however, that God is, even now, the victor:

> "In this world you will have trouble. But take heart! I have overcome the orld" (John 16:33).
>
> "For the Lord your God is the one who goes with you to fight for you against your enemies to give you victory" (Deuteronomy 20:4).
>
> "Do not be afraid or discouraged because of this vast army. For the battle is not yours, but God's" (2 Chronicles 20:15).

Nonetheless, we should take Jesus' words, "watch and pray," fully to heart. Doing so is fundamental to following God's call: "For though we live in the world, we do not wage war as the world does. The weapons we fight with are not the weapons of the world. On the contrary, they have divine power to demolish strongholds" (2 Corinthians 10:3–4).

And our watching will be more effective if we consider in advance some of the traps that could lie before us; that will be our focus over the next few days.

Father God—We come to you excited to carry out your work, to be an active part of your eternal plan, but we know that the path ahead will not be free from trouble. Teach us to rely on you as our guardian and our guide. Keep our spirits alert and watchful, so that we may stay true to your call, no matter how difficult the journey. You are the victor! And we look forward to not only witnessing that victory, but participating in it. In the name of our Lord and Savior, Jesus Christ, we pray. Amen.

Notes

25

ALL MY PRIDE

Pride: *1. The quality or state of being proud: such as (a) inordinate self-esteem: conceit; (b) a reasonable or justifiable self-respect.*
—Merriam-Webster

If anyone slaps you on the right cheek, turn to them the other cheek also. And if anyone wants to sue you and take your shirt, hand over your coat as well. If anyone forces you to go one mile, go with them two miles.
—Matthew 5:39–42

The context of Jesus' words, as recorded in Matthew, is one of Roman occupation. The land that had been promised to the Jewish people so long ago, that was an integral part of their heritage and identity, was under Roman control, along with the people themselves. They, the Jewish people, were the followers of the one true, almighty God, yet they were subject to the authority of a people who paid no heed to their God. Consequently, in this passage in Matthew, Jesus is not describing anomalous incidents, but repeated indignities within an ongoing context of offense. What is the message that he wants to convey?

Let's consider what the three circumstances have in common. In each, the will of one person is imposed upon another. And in each, this imposition is legal but is demeaning to the one being imposed upon. Yet, in all instances, Jesus' instruction is not only to tolerate the offense, but to accept a double portion. Why? What is the objective?

To further our understanding, let's see what this teaching looks like when put into practice:

> "I offered my back to those who beat me, my cheeks to those who pulled out my beard; I did not hide my face from mocking and spitting" (Isaiah 50:6).

> "When they hurled their insults at him, he did not retaliate; when he suffered, he made no threats" (1 Peter 2:23a).

Why would anyone endure this kind of treatment?

"For I have come down from heaven not to do my will but to do the will of him who sent me" (John 6:38).

"By myself I can do nothing; I judge only as I hear, and my judgment is just, for **I seek not to please myself but him who sent me**" (John 5:30; emphasis added).

How does a person make such a choice?

"**Jesus knew that the Father had put all things under his power, and that he had come from God and was returning to God**; so he got up from the meal, took off his outer clothing, and wrapped a towel around his waist. After that, he poured water into a basin and began to wash his disciples' feet, drying them with the towel that was wrapped around him" (John 13:3–5; emphasis added).

"When they hurled their insults at him, he did not retaliate; when he suffered, he made no threats. Instead, **he entrusted himself to him who judges justly**" (1 Peter 2:23; emphasis added).

"And being found in appearance as a man, **he humbled himself** by becoming obedient to death—even death on a cross!" (Philippians 2:7–8; emphasis added).

Now we have our answer. What is Jesus saying in Matthew 5? God comes first. His interests come first. His will comes first. His kingdom comes first. Not only first, but last and middle also. There is no room for personal pride when doing God's work, only humility. Why?

Because pride is focused on self, while humility is focused on God and others. Pride wants to do things "my (or our) way," while humility wants to do things God's way. Pride wants to be the recipient of gratitude, while humility is grateful for the opportunity to do God's work. Pride wants to be the recipient of praise, while humility wants to bring glory and praise to God. Pride is quick to feel wounded and defensive, while humility is secure in God's care. Pride goes to great lengths to avoid being ill-used, while humility goes to great lengths to be useful. Pride is fearful, while humility is courageous. And pride is quick to retaliate, while humility is quick to seek God's will.

Does Jesus' teaching in Matthew mean that we should not work to rid the world of injustice and oppression? Certainly not! God makes his will clear on these matters (see Isaiah 58). But we do so not out of a desire for retribution, but out of a desire for redemption for all. And we don't draw from a well of hate, but from a well of love. It is not self-interest, but God's will, that determines our actions, and he is the one who guides us.

And does putting God first mean that we view ourselves as having no worth? As having no dignity? On the contrary! We are children of the Almighty God! We are the brothers and sisters of Christ! That is where our worth, our dignity, resides: with God. God does not desire for us to endure abusive or harmful relationships,* but neither do we have to prove or defend our self-worth; it is wholly secure and unassailable. In this way, we are liberated to do God's will fully, without being fettered by self-interest.

In other words:

> "Whoever wants to be my disciple must deny themselves and take up their cross daily and follow me" (Luke 9:23).

> "For whoever does the will of my Father in heaven is my brother and sister and mother" (Matthew 12:50).

How often do we see triumph where God sees loss? How often do we see loss where God sees triumph? Jesus calls us to see differently, to understand differently. We cannot serve two masters. Will we nail our pride to the cross? Or our God? This is a choice that we make, repeatedly, every single day.

Almighty God—You call us to entrust ourselves fully to you so that we can live fully for you. But honestly, this call goes against every fiber of our beings. So often, throughout any given day, the innate desire to preserve our own sense of worth, our self-respect, our basic human dignity drives our decisions. Teach us to turn to you, not just first, but instead. Teach us to follow your lead, unswayed by self-interest, knowing that you hold our worth, our dignity, securely in your hands. In the name of our Lord and Savior, Jesus Christ, we pray. Amen.

**If you are caught in an abusive or harmful relationship, please call the National Domestic Violence Hotline immediately at 1-800-799-7233, or seek help from a pastor, police officer, or other authority.*

Notes ____

26

LOVE'S LIMITS

But I tell you, love your enemies and pray for those who persecute you, that you may be children of your Father in heaven.
—Matthew 5:44–45

Where does your love reach its limits? What is the obstacle that it can't climb, the line that it can't cross? Who remains outside of its reach?

Perhaps murderers, rapists, or pedophiles? Human traffickers? Terrorists? Perpetrators of genocide?

Maybe athletes who kneel during the national anthem, or those who don't? Tree huggers or climate-change deniers? Racists, bigots? Antifa adherents, Black Lives Matter activists? Republicans or Democrats? Mormons, Muslims, atheists? Or maybe certain Christians?

Or is it more personal? A family member, a friend, a neighbor, someone at work? Maybe even someone at church?

We all have a line beyond which our love doesn't reach. A point beyond which we couldn't extend it even if we wanted to … and in some cases, we really don't want to. This is true of all of us; of you and of me. We're not talking about love in theory or in the abstract, but tangible, practical, I'd-go-to-the-mat-for-you love. Love as a verb, not a noun.

What is it that makes a person unlovable? At what point does flawed become too flawed? How do we differentiate "us" from "them"? Is it that we would never commit such heinous atrocities? We would never hold such uninformed, damaging, foolish, divisive, hateful (pick-your-adjective) views? We would never demean, betray, or hurt someone in such a way? Because we wouldn't. Would we?

As for me, given my condition, I'm certainly in no position to judge.

Each day begins with such good intentions,
only to end with the crucifixion
of my God.

Blood runs thick across my hands,
pooling at my feet while I stand,
guilty as sin.

I fall, stricken, to my knees,
begging for mercy, some reprieve,
though it's not deserved.

No grounds to appeal my just conviction,
I grasp the cup of my shame and perdition,
drawn from life's spill.

And I drink every drop of my damnation,
but find, against all expectation,
life in place of death.

I can't begin to understand
the mystery of this God-become-man
who willingly stretched out his hands in death
to give us life.

But I do know this:
God loves us without condition,
and he fights for us, despite our imperfections.

Do we do the same?

Only one among us has avoided committing heinous atrocities, only one among us has caused no one any harm, only one among us has known and understood perfectly. And he died on a cross … for us … the heinous ones.

What then shall we, his followers, do? Will we stand before his cross and attempt to justify the limitations of our love? Or try to hide them from a God who sees and knows all? What would be gained by doing so? And what lost?

Let's instead come before him, acknowledging and confessing what he already knows: that our love is flawed and weak. That at a certain point, it dries up, it runs out.

For we have a God whose love is perfect and powerful, infinite and unconditional. It is a fountain that never runs dry, that has no limits. This is the love that he has for us, and for all the world through us, if we just ask.

But does this love mean that there is no accountability for wrongs committed, for harm done? Not at all! Accountability is the doorway through which mercy and grace gain their meaning, their existence. To love is to hold accountable when accountability is needed. But love's aim is healing, not hurt; wholeness, not brokenness; redemption, not retribution.

Our God binds the wounds and heals the hurt, he makes shattered lives whole, he redeems the irredeemable. But he does so through us. When he asks, "Whom shall I send?" are we willing to say, "Here am I. Send me!"?

Father God—We confess that our love has limits. We are prone to picking and choosing those who are worthy of it, and even when we don't, it tends to give out where it is, perhaps, most needed. We pray that you will pour your love into us, but don't just fill in where our love leaves off. Don't mix the perfect with the imperfect. Instead, please empty us of our weak, imperfect love; cast it aside so that we are filled entirely with your powerful, perfect love. Love that is life altering and world changing. In the name of our Lord and Savior, Jesus Christ, we pray. Amen.

Notes

27

WE'VE GOT THIS

Shortly before dawn Jesus went out to them, walking on the lake. When the disciples saw him walking on the lake, they were terrified. 'It's a ghost,' they said, and cried out in fear. But Jesus immediately said to them: 'Take courage! It is I. Don't be afraid.' 'Lord, if it's you,' Peter replied, 'tell me to come to you on the water.' 'Come,' he said. Then Peter got down out of the boat, walked on the water and came toward Jesus. But when he saw the wind, he was afraid and, beginning to sink, cried out, 'Lord, save me!' Immediately Jesus reached out his hand and caught him. 'You of little faith,' he said, 'why did you doubt?'
—Matthew 14:25–31

God's mission call can seem so simple at the outset: "Come," he says. Share the gospel in Nepal, help educate children in Haiti, reach out to those trapped in poverty right here, in the local community. No problem, right?

Except, where exactly in Nepal? How do we get to such a remote location? Where will we stay? Who will translate for us? And what will we say? What does "help educate children" mean anyway? What are they lacking? Buildings? Supplies? The required shoes? Qualified teachers? And what does "reaching out" mean? What hurdles are families facing? Which ones are temporary and which ones are enduring? What approach will be most effective? Carried out by whom? What is the best mechanism to meet the need? Are we fostering dependence or independence? Are we building in sustainability? What does God intend our role to be?

The moment we accept God's call, we face a tidal wave of questions. As they say, the devil is in the details, and in missions, that can literally be true. Because as we make the transition from "Here am I. Send me!" to "Now what?" we're prone to making another transition: from "God's got this" to "we've got this"; from God-reliance to self-reliance.

How do we tell the difference? Self-reliance clings to what has worked in the past; God-reliance embraces new possibilities, it builds on past experience without being confined by it. Self-reliance is risk-averse; God-reliance is risk-tolerant. Self-reliance is limited to what we can do; God-reliance is limited to what

God can do (that is, it's unlimited). Self-reliance seeks to make things happen; God-reliance seeks God's guidance and timing. The biggest fear of self-reliance is failure of the mission endeavor; the biggest fear of God-reliance is failure to adhere to God's call.

What does self-reliance look like?

> "The Lord said to Moses, 'Send some men to explore the land of Canaan, which I am giving to the Israelites.' ...So at the Lord's command Moses sent them out from the Desert of Paran. ...They came back to Moses and Aaron and the whole Israelite community ...They gave Moses this account: 'We went into the land to which you sent us, and it does flow with milk and honey! Here is its fruit. But the people who live there are powerful, and the cities are fortified and very large. ...We can't attack those people; they are stronger than we are.' And they spread among the Israelites a bad report about the land they had explored" (Numbers 13:1–3, 26–28, 31–32).

And God-reliance?

> "Then Joshua son of Nun secretly sent two spies from Shittim. 'Go, look over the land,' he said, 'especially Jericho.' So they went and entered the house of a prostitute named Rahab and stayed there. ...When they left, they went into the hills and stayed there three days ... Then the two men started back. ... They said to Joshua, 'The Lord has surely given the whole land into our hands; all the people are melting in fear because of us'" (Joshua 2:1, 22–24).

But shouldn't we aim to be well prepared for God's mission? Shouldn't we draw upon the best knowledge, skillsets, talents, and gifts available? Shouldn't we apply wisdom and discernment? By all means! Doing so makes us well-equipped and well-informed. Who we then rely on is a separate matter.

If we choose to be well-equipped, well-informed, and self-reliant, we will never escape the confines of our own limitations. But if we choose to be well-equipped, well-informed, and God-reliant, we will see God's promises fulfilled (see Days 19–23).

As church members, are we willing to rely on God? Are we willing to follow his call, wherever it leads? Are we willing to rearrange our priorities and our lives to suit his needs? Are we willing to step beyond what we can do, and into what he can do?

For those who are church leaders, are we growing the God-reliance of our members? Are we hesitant to ask too much of them? Do we wrap missions in risk-free, success-guaranteed packages? Do we make sure that the missions vision we present seems readily doable? Do we tend to automatically adhere to the decisions and approaches of the past?

Or do we ask much of our members? Are we willing to draw them beyond the comfort zone into the faith zone? Are we willing to present a missions vision that is dauntingly big and demanding, and maybe even different from anything we've done before? What do we fear more: a missions effort that fails outwardly, or a missions effort that fails inwardly (asks too little of our members, requires no increase in faith)? Whereas the former represents a temporary setback, on which God can readily build, the latter represents long-term disaster.

God is always moving forward; change, not stasis, is the status quo. He invites us to join him on a mission that is bigger, bolder, more daunting, more difficult, and more ridiculously unachievable (by us) than we can even begin to comprehend. He calls us to do not what we can do, but what he can do. He calls us to "Come." The only thing standing in our way is us.

Almighty God—Your mission began before time itself. We cannot begin to grasp the scope of it, the depth of it, the complexity of it. Yet, despite our many limitations, you call on us to join you, to be a part of your work. To live beyond ourselves through you. Draw us close to rest in your embrace, to reside in your Spirit. Strengthen our resolve and deepen our faith, so that when you say, "Come," we will follow, uncowed by the depth of the water or the height of the waves. In the name of our Lord and Savior, Jesus Christ, we pray. Amen.

Notes

28

EARTHLY MEASURES

"Trust in the Lord with all your heart and lean not on your own understanding; in all your ways submit to him, and he will make your paths straight."
—Proverbs 3:5–6

"Let us not become weary in doing good, for at the proper time we will reap a harvest if we do not give up."
—Galatians 6:9

Why do we do missions? Why do we devote ourselves—our time, talent, energy, skills, knowledge, resources—to carrying out God's work?

Is it out of a sense of duty to God, given all that he has done for us? Out of love, in response to his great love for us? Is it in recognition of the fact that all that we are comes from him anyway, and is meant to be used for his purposes? All of the above?

But what if we pour ourselves into a missions endeavor, and the anticipated results are not forthcoming? Does it matter? Would we consider the effort a failure? A waste of our investment? Let's consider a few examples.

- In 1912, a man named Dr. William Leslie went to a remote area of the Democratic Republic of Congo (then called the Belgian Congo) as a missionary to the Yansi people. After 17 years, he left, convinced that he had failed to make any impact for Christ.

- Jim Elliot was called to Ecuador to reach the Auca people, located deep in the jungle. He and four other missionaries had a positive initial meeting with a few members of the tribe. However, when they returned for a second meeting, they were attacked, and all five missionaries were killed.

- The date of Christianity's arrival in India may have been as early as the first century A.D., or as late as the sixth or seventh century. Either way, Christianity has had a presence in India for more than two millennia. Yet according to official census numbers, Christians constitute only about 2.3 percent of the total population of India (given the hesitancy of some to openly indicate their Christian faith, it's possible the share is closer to 6 percent; still low for two thousand years' worth of work).

If we were the ones supporting or carrying out these missions, would we forge ahead or pull the plug? Would we see these missions as successes or failures? Based on what?

What mindset do we bring to missions? Is it a secular one? Does the inception and continuation of a mission hinge on its return on investment? Will its success be judged based on quantifiable results tied to previously defined key indicators? Are milestones established that must be reached within a particular time frame? Is our functioning assumption that, if the mission is in response to God's call, the anticipated results (as we define them) will automatically be forthcoming? Does our mindset have something of a prosperity-gospel bent?

At the most fundamental level, why do we do missions? For the results? Or for God?

It's not that results don't matter, or that progress shouldn't be measured. But we must make these assessments within an entirely different framework from that of secular endeavors, as evidenced by the question at the start of all that we do: What is God's call?

That first question is quickly followed by three more: Are we adhering to God's call? Are we doing so with the utmost integrity? And are we doing so as effectively as possible? This last one is where the measurements and assessments come in handy, as long as they are kept in their proper place, subordinate to God's call.

Why is this important? Because the secular approach assumes that we fully understand the mission. That we know what the results are supposed to be. That we are the ones in control. But with missions, the truth is that we know very little. We know (or have some sense of) what God has called us to do, but not much beyond that.

- What is the timeline, truly, when all is said and done? God only knows.

- Does the mission represent God's singular objective? Or is it only one component of many? Is it perhaps not even the primary one? God only knows.

- Is God's focus primarily on the mission's direct results? Or will there be indirect consequences (ripple effects), that in hindsight, will prove to be of greater import? God only knows.

- In calling us to a particular mission, is God's primary aim to reach a certain group of people? Or is it to reach, teach, and grow us, his Church? Or both? God only knows.

As Dr. Leslie departed the Belgian Congo, as the team of missionaries was killed in Ecuador, what did God know that those missionaries could not? What was the rest of the story?

- In 2010, a missions team made the trek to the villages of the Yansi people in the Democratic Republic of Congo. The team anticipated that the people might have heard of Jesus but would have little knowledge beyond that. To their amazement, they discovered a network of churches, one in each village. There was even a 1,000-seat stone "cathedral" in one village. Each village also had a gospel choir, and they would write their own songs and have sing-offs between villages. What had seemed like 17 years of abject failure had, in fact, produced abundant fruit, but no one knew it for more than 80 years.

- In Ecuador, Jim Elliot's wife, Elisabeth, renewed contact with the Auca people. A couple of years after her husband's death, she and her 3-year-old daughter, along with the sister of one of the previous missionaries, moved in with the Aucas. Their ministry helped break the cycle of violence within the community and resulted in numerous conversions. But that was only the beginning, because Elisabeth went on to capture the story of the five missionary men in *Through Gates of Splendor,* and the story of her husband's life and work in *Shadow of the Almighty,* both of which became influential bestsellers. She went on to write 24 books in total; traveled across the United States, sharing her story; and hosted a radio program aimed at women. She was considered by many to be one of the most influential Christian women of the 20th century.

- India's story is ongoing, but what do we know so far? A share of 2.3 percent of the population equals roughly 28 million people. If we assume that the share of Christians is closer to 6 percent, then that comes to roughly 84 million people. Either way, many millions of people have received the gift of eternal life thanks to missions efforts, and that's taking into account only the present day. Yes, the share is only 2–6 percent. That just means there's a lot of room for great things yet to come.

In missions, what we don't know exceeds what we know. God is the one with the complete picture, the one in control, the one with the answers. So in the end, the key question is this: Why do we do missions? For the results, as we define them? Or for God? When the going gets tough, is the latter enough?

> "He is no fool who gives what he cannot keep to gain what he cannot lose" (Jim Elliot).

> "Fear arises when we imagine that everything depends on us" (Elisabeth Elliot).

Almighty God—We have a need to prove that what we're doing is worthwhile, that we're not being foolish. But you call us to be fools for you. Let our spirits be attuned to your call, and when we hear it, compel us to follow it heedlessly … yes, even foolishly. Instill within us the deep-seated conviction that, as long as we adhere to your call, every investment we make is worthwhile, even when all evidence points to the contrary. In the name of our Lord and Savior, Jesus Christ, we pray. Amen.

Sources:
William Leslie: http://blog.godreports.com/2014/05/missionary-died-thinking-he-was-a-failure-84-years-later-thriving-churches-found-hidden-in-the-jungle/
Elisabeth Elliot: https://www.thegospelcoalition.org/article/9-things-you-should-know-about-elisabeth-elliot/
Jim Elliot: https://www.thegospelcoalition.org/blogs/justin-taylor/they-were-no-fools-60-years-ago-today-the-martyrdom-of-jim-elliot-and-four-other-missionaries/
India: https://www.outlookindia.com/magazine/story/why-christianity-failed-in-india/293895

Notes

Prayer and Meditation

29

GOD SPEAKS

As we wind down this series of devotions, we enter a time of reflection and prayer. Today, we focus on God's message to his people (his church), recorded in Isaiah 58. We've previously delved into portions of this passage, but a full hearing is due. So today, God speaks, pouring out his mind and his heart in a message that conveys the uncompromising expectations of God our Father; the gracious, sacrificial love of God the Son; and the powerful, renewing force of God the Spirit.

What does your spirit hear in the voice of our triune God? What resonates? What challenges? What convicts? What affirms? What inspires?

We come into your presence, Holy Father, Son, and Spirit. Tune our spirits to your voice:

"Shout it aloud, do not hold back.
Raise your voice like a trumpet.
Declare to my people their rebellion
and to the descendants of Jacob their sins.
For day after day they seek me out;
they seem eager to know my ways,
as if they were a nation that does what is right
and has not forsaken the commands of its God.
They ask me for just decisions
and seem eager for God to come near them.
'Why have we fasted,' they say,
'and you have not seen it?
Why have we humbled ourselves,
and you have not noticed?'

"Yet on the day of your fasting, you do as you please
and exploit all your workers.
Your fasting ends in quarreling and strife,
and in striking each other with wicked fists.
You cannot fast as you do today
and expect your voice to be heard on high.
Is this the kind of fast I have chosen,

only a day for people to humble themselves?
Is it only for bowing one's head like a reed
and for lying in sackcloth and ashes?
Is that what you call a fast,
a day acceptable to the Lord?

"Is not this the kind of fasting I have chosen:
to loose the chains of injustice
and untie the cords of the yoke,
to set the oppressed free
and break every yoke?
Is it not to share your food with the hungry
and to provide the poor wanderer with shelter—
when you see the naked, to clothe them,
and not to turn away from your own flesh and blood?
Then your light will break forth like the dawn,
and your healing will quickly appear;
then your righteousness will go before you,
and the glory of the Lord will be your rear guard.
Then you will call, and the Lord will answer;
you will cry for help, and he will say: Here am I.

If you do away with the yoke of oppression,
with the pointing finger and malicious talk,
and if you spend yourselves in behalf of the hungry
and satisfy the needs of the oppressed,
then your light will rise in the darkness,
and your night will become like the noonday.
The Lord will guide you always;
he will satisfy your needs in a sun-scorched land
and will strengthen your frame.
You will be like a well-watered garden,
like a spring whose waters never fail.
Your people will rebuild the ancient ruins
and will raise up the age-old foundations;
you will be called Repairer of Broken Walls,
Restorer of Streets with Dwellings.

"If you keep your feet from breaking the Sabbath
and from doing as you please on my holy day,
if you call the Sabbath a delight
and the Lord's holy day honorable,
and if you honor it by not going your own way

and not doing as you please or speaking idle words,
then you will find your joy in the Lord,
and I will cause you to ride in triumph on the heights of the land
and to feast on the inheritance of your father Jacob."
For the mouth of the Lord has spoken.

Almighty God—May your words resonate within us, may they reverberate through our hearts and minds. May our spirits sing at the sound of your voice. May our lives ignite with your unquenchable, holy fire. Revive us, oh, Lord, and through us, the world. In the name of our Lord and Savior, Jesus Christ, we pray. Amen.

Notes

30

CATCHING THE VISION

Do not conform to the pattern of this world, but be transformed by the renewing of your mind. Then you will be able to test and approve what God's will is—his good, pleasing and perfect will.
—*Romans 12:2*

Yesterday, we listened to God speak through Isaiah 58. Today, we more fully immerse ourselves into a time of prayer and reflection. Consider the questions below in light of God's message to his people, to us, in Isaiah 58. What is God speaking into your life? Into our lives, collectively? What is his vision for you? For us?

Father God—You promise that those who seek will find. We earnestly seek your voice, your message, your vision as we reflect on the questions below. Open our eyes, Lord, to the reality of what is and your promise of what could be. Reveal to us your will for our lives, for the local church, and for your universal Church. In Jesus' name we pray. Amen.

Questions for Personal, Prayerful Reflection:
Thinking in specific, concrete terms, what lies in ruins today? What land has become sun-scorched? (Isaiah 58:11–12)

- Within my life?
- Within my family?
- Within this community?
- Within this nation?
- Within the world?
- Within the local church?
- Within God's universal Church?

God promises a return to Eden, a new Jerusalem, when we live within his will. What does it mean to be a well-watered garden, a restored city? What are the key features? What is different from the way things are now? What is the same?

- Within my life?
- Within my family?
- Within this community?

- Within this nation?
- Within the world?
- Within the local church?
- Within God's universal Church?

What changes do I/we need to make to see God's promises fulfilled? What does it mean to commit to the fast that God has chosen (Isaiah 58:6–7)? What would we do less of or eliminate entirely? What would we start doing or do more of? What would we prioritize differently?

- Thinking in terms of myself?
- My family?
- The local church?
- God's universal Church?

Be Thou my Vision, O Lord of my heart;
Naught be all else to me, save that Thou art.
Thou my best Thought, by day or by night,
Waking or sleeping, Thy presence my light.

Be Thou my Wisdom, Thou my true Word;
I ever with Thee and Thou with me, Lord;
Thou my great Father, I Thy dear son;
Thou in me dwelling, I with Thee one.

Be Thou my battle Shield, sword for the fight;
Be Thou my dignity, Thou my delight;
Thou my soul's shelter, Thou my high tower:
Raise Thou me heavenward, Power of my power.

Riches I heed not, nor man's empty praise,
Thou mine inheritance, now and always:
Thou, and Thou only, first in my heart,
High King of Heaven, my Treasure Thou art.

With the High King of Heaven, after victory won,
May I reach heaven's joys, O bright heaven's Sun!
Heart of my own heart, whatever befall,
Still be my Vision, O Ruler of all.

In the name of our Lord and Savior, Jesus Christ, we pray. Amen.

Song cited: "Be Thou My Vision," attributed to Dallan Forgaill, 8th century; translation by Mary Byrne (1905), versified by Eleanor Hull (1912). Public domain.

Invitation

31

GOD'S WILL, OUR WILLINGNESS

Therefore, since we are surrounded by such a great cloud of witnesses, let us throw off everything that hinders and the sin that so easily entangles. And let us run with perseverance the race marked out for us, fixing our eyes on Jesus, the pioneer and perfecter of faith.
—Hebrews 12:1–2

When we become followers of Christ, we also become ambassadors for Christ, representing him in all that we say and do. We gain an eternal mission, his mission: to tend to the need, both temporal and eternal; to work for restoration of both body and soul. For most of us, our call is not to distant lands or history-making endeavors. We are ordinary, everyday Christians, called to be missionaries-in-place.

Our mission field is school, work, the neighborhoods in which we live, the stores that we frequent. From the moment we step out of bed to the moment we crawl back in, we are on mission, in every encounter, every conversation, every attitude, word, and action. Our missions call might not be a paid vocation, but it is full time.

Questions for Personal, Prayerful Reflection:
What stands in the way of our fully embracing God's call? What prevents us from committing to his fast and seeing his promises fulfilled?

- Thinking in terms of myself?
- My family?
- The local church?

How can these impediments be overcome? What changes could I make? What changes could we make, together?

- For myself?
- Within my family?
- Within the local church?

Missions is the convergence of God's will and our willingness. God's will is ever-present. That leaves only one question: Are we willing?

Father God—Instill within us a deep-seated desire to dedicate our lives to you, every moment of every day. May your fast become our fast, may your mission be our mission. May you be the fulcrum of our lives, the linchpin that holds everything else in its rightful place. May we become, individually and collectively, all that you created us to be. In the name of our Lord and Savior, Jesus Christ, we pray. Amen.

Notes

Benediction

32

GOD'S BREATH

And we all, who with unveiled faces contemplate the Lord's glory, are being transformed into his image with ever-increasing glory, which comes from the Lord, who is the Spirit.
—2 Corinthians 3:18

We began this series of devotions by looking at God's example of what being on mission means, and then we proceeded to explore who we are in God's eyes. From there we asked, so what? What difference does this make in our lives? We then delved into a few of God's extraordinary promises to his people, promises that come to fruition when we carry out his will, and then we studied some of the "mission traps" that can lead us astray. Finally, we immersed ourselves in prayer and meditation, seeking God's will for ourselves, our local churches, and his universal Church.

As you reflect on the journey we've taken together, and as you ponder the journey yet to come, receive this benediction:

May God lead you down paths you could never have found, to places you could never have imagined. May his abundant love pour into you and through you, the overflow spilling into the lives of all whom you encounter.

Where your life is broken, may the shards form a lens of compassion through which to view the brokenness of others. May there be no hurt, no heartache, no hardship that you do not feel as your own. In the imperfections of others, may you see your own reflection, and in their potential, may you see the image of God.

May God give you his eyes, to see through what is, to the possibility of what could be. May he give you his heart, to love even when (especially when) love seems impossible. May he give you his Spirit, to draw you close, so that when people see you, they see him.

May you live large, unassailable in the confidence that you are a child of God, for now and forever. May he surround you with his presence, paving the way before you and defending you from behind. May your faith be unwavering and ever-growing. May it never falter, though all else fails. May the assurance of God-with-Us be the rock on which you stand and your shelter in the storm.

May the unstoppable, life-giving stream of God's Spirit nourish and strengthen you. May you be a well-watered garden to all who encounter you: a source of refreshment, of renewal, of vibrant, abundant life. May the seeds of peace, harmony, and love sprout and flourish in your wake.

May you be a new Jerusalem: for those who are lost, a place of welcome; for those who despair, a source of hope; for those who are hurting, a source of comfort; for those who are broken, a source of restoration; and for those who are dying, a source of Life.

May your life be transcendent. May the impact of the words you speak, the choices you make, and the actions you take make a difference not only for today, but for all eternity. And when the time comes, may you hear the words, "Well done, good and faithful servant" (Matthew 25:23).

In the name of our Lord and Savior, Jesus Christ. Amen.

Notes

Special thanks to Vienna Presbyterian Church for the vision and encouragement to publish this devotional.

Belong!
neighbors loving neighbors

Recommended Reading

- *The Hole in Our Gospel: What Does God Expect of Us?* by Richard Stearns
- *To Alter Your World: Partnering with God to Rebirth our Communities* by Michael Frost and Christiana Rice
- *Helping Without Hurting in Church Benevolence* by Steve Corbett and Brian Fikkert, or related videos at the Chalmers Center website: www.chalmers.org/the-small group-experience
- *The Cost of Discipleship* by Dietrich Bonhoeffer

Notes

51285895R00049

Made in the USA
Middletown, DE
01 July 2019